HOW DOES IT WORK?

How Does a JET PLANE Work?

BY SARAH EASON

Gareth Stevens
Publishing

Please visit our Web site www.garethstevens.com. For a free color catalog of all our high-quality books, call toll free 1-800-542-2595 or fax 1-877-542-2596.

Library of Congress Cataloging-in-Publication Data
Eason, Sarah.
How does a jet plane work? / Sarah Eason.
p. cm. -- (How does it work?)
Includes bibliographical references and index.
ISBN 978-1-4339-3471-1 (library binding) -- ISBN 978-1-4339-3472-8 (pbk.)
ISBN 978-1-4339-3473-5 (6-pack)
1. Jet planes--Juvenile literature. I. Title.
TL709.E323 2010
629.133'349--dc22   2009039328

Published in 2010 by
Gareth Stevens Publishing
111 East 14th Street, Suite 349
New York, NY 10003

© 2010 The Brown Reference Group Ltd.

For Gareth Stevens Publishing:
Art Direction: Haley Harasymiw
Editorial Direction: Kerri O'Donnell

For The Brown Reference Group Ltd:
Editorial Director: Lindsey Lowe
Managing Editor: Tim Harris
Editor: Sarah Eason
Children's Publisher: Anne O'Daly
Design Manager: David Poole
Designer: Paul Myerscough
Production Director: Alastair Gourlay

Picture Credits:
Front cover: Shutterstock: Ajak Bhaskar (background); Brown Reference Group (foreground)

Illustrations by Roger Courthold and Mark Walker

Picture Credits Key: t – top, b – below, c – center, l – left, r – right. NASA: 29; Shutterstock: ABC Photo 22, Katrina Brown 24, Clara 20, Dr Flash 25, Chris H Galbraith 23b, Ivan Cholakov Gostock 7, 8–9, Gudmund 17, Khafizov Ivan Harisovich 11t, David Hernandez 13b, Barry Maas 16, Charles F McCarthy 26, Mamel 10, MaxFX 18, Thomas O'Neil 27t, PerWil 21t, Phantom 14–15, Dan Simonsen 19b, Thor Jorgen Udvang 12, Brad Whitsitt 6; U.S. Air Force: 28

Publisher's note to educators and parents: Our editors have carefully reviewed the Web sites that appear on p. 31 to ensure that they are suitable for students. Many Web sites change frequently, however, and we cannot guarantee that a site's future contents will continue to meet our high standards of quality and educational value. Be advised that students should be closely supervised whenever they access the Internet.

Printed in the United States of America
1 2 3 4 5 6 7 8 9   12 11 10

CPSIA compliance information: Batch #BRW0102GS: For further information contact Gareth Stevens, New York, New York at 1-800-542-2595.

Contents

How Does a Jet Plane Work?   4

History of Jet Planes   6

How Planes Fly   8

What Is a Jet Engine?   10

Different Jet Engines   12

Flying Faster   14

In the Cockpit   16

Life in the Clouds   18

Staying Safe   20

Finding the Way   22

Building a Jet Plane   24

Military Jets   26

The Future of Jet Planes   28

Glossary   30

Further Information   31

Index   32

How Does a Jet Plane Work?

Passenger airliners are huge planes. They can carry hundreds of passengers at a time and travel thousands of miles across the globe. Most passenger airplanes are Boeing 747s, or "jumbo jets."

Most passengers sit in the main cabin.

Flaps extend up and down to slow the airplane.

The aileron steers the airplane by making it roll from side to side.

The spoiler sticks up during landing to slow the airplane.

An antenna picks up radio signals from airports and other airplanes.

Anti-collision lights flash to make the airplane stand out in the dark.

The crew controls the plane from the flight deck.

A weather radar system in the nose tells the crew about the weather ahead.

Some passengers sit on the upper deck.

Bright landing lights on the wings illuminate the runway during takeoff and landing.

Fast Facts

The Airbus A380, or "Superjumbo," is currently the biggest passenger jet plane in the world.

The fuselage is made of an aluminum frame. It is covered with a "skin" of thin metal panels.

The rudder moves from left to right to steer the airplane.

The elevator on the tailplane makes the airplane pitch up and down.

The cargo is loaded into the hold through the freight door under the aircraft.

The landing gear engages the wheels to land the plane.

The flaps move along fairings attached to the underside of the wings.

Boeing 747s have four turbofan engines.

Raising the winglet makes the plane more stable in bad weather.

5

History of Jet Planes

The earliest airplanes were driven by propellers. They were slow compared to airplanes powered by jet engines.

The first airplane took to the skies in 1903. It was called *Flyer,* and it was invented by American brothers Orville (1871–1948) and Wilbur Wright (1867–1912). Over the next 25 years, aircraft designers made improvements to the design of aircraft.

Fun Facts

German pilots who flew the German Me 262 said the jet engines felt "like angels pushing" the aircraft because it was moving so fast—nearly 550 miles (880 km) per hour.

An artist's impression shows what Orville and Wilbur Wright's plane, *Flyer,* would have looked like in flight.

When British engineer Frank Whittle (1907–1996) invented the jet engine in 1930, aircraft engineers raced to make the first jet-powered plane. By the start of World War II (1939–1945), German engineer Hans Pabst von Ohain (1911–1998) had built the first jet plane. Later in the war, the German Messerschmitt Me 262 became the first jet plane to enter military service.

Two Russian MiG jet fighter planes fly in formation.

Air travel

After the war, aircraft engineers built jet planes for passenger flights. The first passenger jet aircraft was the de Havilland Comet, which started flying between Britain and South Africa in 1952. PanAm started the first transatlantic service in 1958 between New York and Paris, France.

Faster than sound

Supersonic jet planes can fly faster than the speed of sound. The first pilot to break the sound barrier was American pilot Chuck Yeager (1923–). In 1947, Yeager flew the rocket-powered Bell X-1 at 807.2 miles (1,299 km) per hour. The Russian MiG-25 is the world's fastest jet. It can fly at speeds over 2,110 miles (3,395 km) per hour.

How Planes Fly

The Boeing 747 "jumbo jet" is a massive machine. It is about 230 feet (70 m) long, weighs more than 387 tons (350 t), and is as tall as a six-story building. How does this massive machine get off the ground and fly in the sky?

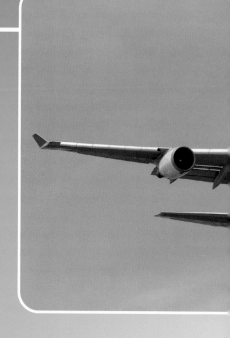

Flight forces

1 The airfoil shape creates a lift force that pushes up on the wing.

2 Four forces act on a plane in flight: thrust, drag, lift, and weight.

3 Control surfaces on the wings and tailplane move to change the forces acting on the plane.

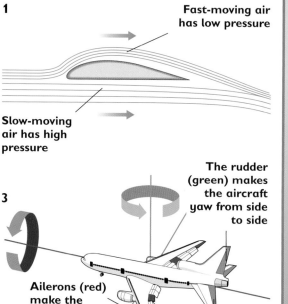

1

Fast-moving air has low pressure

Slow-moving air has high pressure

The rudder (green) makes the aircraft yaw from side to side

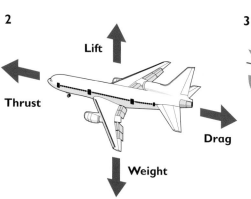

2

Lift

Thrust

Drag

Weight

3

Ailerons (red) make the aircraft roll

Elevators (blue) make the aircraft pitch up and down

A Boeing 747 comes in for a landing. The pilot reduces the speed of the plane so its weight pushing down is greater than the lift force pushing up.

When a plane takes off, all of the engine's power is used to generate a huge lift force. The lift force is greater than the plane's weight. The plane rises into the air. When the plane lands, the pilot reduces the speed. The plane's weight is then greater than the lift force. The plane sinks to the ground. Forces called thrust and drag also act on a plane in flight. Thrust is the forward force created by the engines. Drag is the backward force caused by air rubbing against the plane's surface.

Lift force

When a plane is moving along, the shape of the wing means that air flowing over the wing travels farther than the air under the wing. The faster-moving air above the wing has a lower pressure than the slower-moving air below the wing. This creates the lift that pushes the aircraft up into the air.

Flight forces

When a jet plane flies in a horizontal line, the lift force balances the weight of the plane pushing down.

Fast Facts

- The weight of an object is the force of gravity pulling down on the object's mass.
- The wings of a jumbo jet are more than 190 feet (58 m) long.

What Is a Jet Engine?

A jet engine creates a stream of hot gas that shoots out of the back of the engine at high speed to push the airplane forward.

Jet engines create a powerful force called thrust to move airplanes forward. The way this works is called action and reaction. Jet engines burn a mixture of fuel and air. This produces exhaust gases that shoot out of the back of the engine. This action pushes the airplane forward with a thrust force, or reaction.

Inside a turbofan engine

The turbofan engine is one of three main types of jet engines. It has a powerful fan at the front that sucks in cold air. A device called a compressor squeezes some of the air into a combustion chamber. The air then mixes with a fuel called kerosene. When the air/fuel mixture burns, it produces exhaust gases that shoot over a turbine. The stream of exhaust gases makes the blades of the turbine spin like a windmill. The exhaust

Two turbofan engines are attached to the wing of this Boeing 747. The fans can be seen inside the jet engines.

A turbofan engine is stripped of its outer bodywork so that repairs can be carried out.

gases then pass out of a nozzle at the back of the engine.

Turbofan types

In one type of turbofan engine, most of the cold air bypasses the compressor and shoots straight out the back of the engine. This is known as a high-bypass turbofan. It is efficient, but limits airplanes to speeds slower than the speed of sound. In a low-bypass turbofan, most of the cold air goes into the compressor. These engines can be used to fly airplanes faster than the speed of sound.

TRY FOR YOURSELF

Try this experiment to see how action and reaction produce a forward thrust like a jet airplane.

You will need:
• thick straw • thread • sticky tape
• balloon • friend

1 Push the thread through the straw. Stick strips of tape to the straw as shown.

2 Blow up a balloon. Hold the neck to keep the air in. Stick the balloon to the straw with the tape.

3 Hold the balloon and one end of the thread. Ask a friend to pull on the other end of thread until it is tight. Let the balloon go. Watch it speed along the thread toward your friend.

The force of the air rushing out of the neck pushes the balloon forward. This is how the exhaust gases in a jet engine push the airplane forward.

Different Jet Engines

There are three different types of jet engines: turbofan/turbojet, turboprop, and ramjet. The most common type of jet engine is the turbofan.

Different jet engines have different uses. Some are designed for passenger airliners, and others for military jet planes. Some are very efficient, while others produce a lot of thrust.

Turbofans and turbojets

Turbofans have fans that blow air into a compressor. They are more fuel-efficient and quieter than turbojets. Turbojets do not have fans to blow air into a compressor. They are more powerful than turbofans and make airplanes fly faster.

Turboprops

Turboprops are jet engines with propellers (instead of fans) at the front. The propeller works like

Many smaller jet aircraft use turboprop jet engines.

the fan of a turbofan engine. It pushes air into a compressor. The rotating propeller creates extra thrust by pushing air around the engine. Turboprops are very efficient, but they can only make airplanes fly at subsonic speeds (below the speed of sound).

Ramjets

Ramjets do not have a compressor. Instead, the engine is shaped to squeeze and slow down air flowing through it. A pump sprays fuel into the ramjet, and the exhaust gases shoot out of the back. Ramjets are simple—little more than an open pipe in which fuel is burned. However, they use a lot of fuel. Ramjets are used to power missiles rather than airplanes.

Types of jet engines

In a turbofan, some air passes into the compressor in the center of the engine and burns with the fuel. Cool air also passes around the center of the engine.

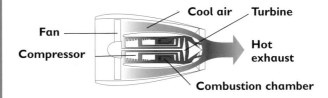

In a turboprop, the propeller provides extra thrust.

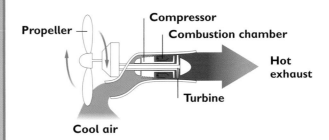

A ramjet is a simple engine that burns fuel in a jet of air.

THAT'S AMAZING!

Most jet engines direct the exhaust gases behind the plane to push it forward. The engines of the Harrier Jump Jet can turn so the nozzles point down, allowing it to take off like a helicopter. Once airborne, the nozzles turn back and the Harrier flies off like a normal plane.

Exhaust nozzle

Flying Faster

Ever since the first plane was built in 1903, airplanes have been getting faster. Modern jet planes can fly many times faster than the speed of sound.

The Russian MiG-25 is the world's fastest jet aircraft.

The speed of sound is not fixed. It changes as the air temperature changes. So the speed of sound is different at different altitudes (height above sea level). At sea level, temperatures are around 60°F (15°C).

Wing shapes

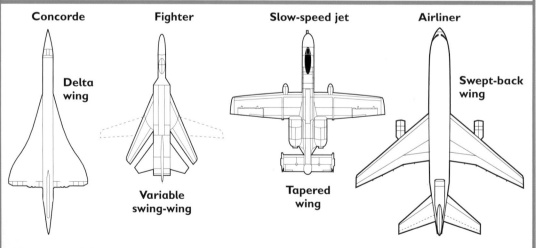

Concorde

Delta wing

Fighter

Variable swing-wing

Slow-speed jet

Tapered wing

Airliner

Swept-back wing

The shape of the wings limits the speed of an airplane. Supersonic aircraft have triangular delta wings. Swept-back wings allow planes to fly just below the speed of sound. Airplanes with tapered wings fly at lower speeds.

The speed of sound at sea level is about 760 miles (1,225 km) per hour. Most jets travel at an altitude between 36,000 and 65,600 feet (11,000 and 20,000 m). Temperatures at this altitude can be as low as −70°F (−57°C). The speed of sound drops to about 660 miles (1,060 km) per hour.

Supersonic airplanes

The fastest jet plane, the MiG-25, flies at 2,110 miles (3,395 km) per hour—more than three times the speed of sound. The Concorde was the fastest passenger jet airliner. It flew at 1,350 miles (2,170 km) per hour—twice the speed of sound.

Shock waves

When supersonic engines break the sound barrier, they create a shock wave. This is heard as a very loud noise called a sonic boom. It can shake the ground below, which can be unpleasant for people. Passengers in the plane cannot hear the sonic

Measuring sound

You can figure out how far away a thunderstorm is using the speed of sound. Count the number of seconds between the flash of lightning and the crack of thunder, divide the number by five, and the result is the distance to the thunderstorm in miles (that's because sound travels at roughly one mile every five seconds at sea level).

Sonic booms

1 As planes fly, they make waves in the air. The waves spread out like ripples on the surface of a pond. Our ears can hear these waves as the plane flies through the sky.

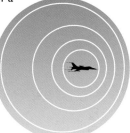

2 When the plane reaches the speed of sound, the waves cannot spread out. They form a huge shock wave. Our ears hear a crack of noise called a sonic boom.

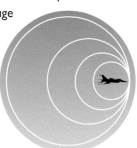

boom, because they are traveling in front of the sound waves the plane creates.

In the Cockpit

The pilot and copilot steer and control the plane, check the flight path, and ensure that all the systems are working. They do this from the cockpit—the nerve center of the airplane.

Control columns are used to steer the plane. There are two control columns—one for the pilot and one for the copilot. Turning the control column left or right moves the ailerons on the wings.

Control column   Rudder pedals   Artificial horizon   Navigation computer   Cabin controls   Engine information   Engine-power controls

The cockpit of a modern jet contains the controls the pilot uses to fly the airplane.

This makes the airplane roll left or right. Moving the control column backward or forward moves the elevators on the tailplane. This makes the airplane rise and fall. Pedals in front of the pilot and copilot move the rudder on the tail. This makes the airplane swing left or right. The panel between the pilot and copilot is used to control the engine's power.

Cockpit control

The cockpit is full of display panels to tell the pilot how the plane is flying. A compass helps the pilot and copilot to fly in the right direction. The artificial horizon tells the pilot and copilot if they are flying level, climbing, or diving. An altimeter shows the plane's altitude. The air-speed indicator shows how fast air is moving past the plane. Computers calculate the speed of the aircraft using data from the altimeter and air-speed indicator. Computers control many of the instruments in a modern jet plane.

The pilot steers the plane using the control column.

THAT'S AMAZING!

When the pilot moves the control column to steer the plane, the movement sends a signal to an electric motor. The motor uses wires to move the control surfaces on the wings and tail. A computer continually adjusts the control surfaces to keep the airplane on course. This system is called fly-by-wire.

Life in the Clouds

When a fighter pilot flies high in the sky, there is less oxygen in the air. Extreme forces act on the body as the pilot twists and dives. High-speed flight can therefore be very uncomfortable—even for experienced pilots.

Passenger jets fly at about 40,000 feet (12,000 m) above the ground. There the air temperature is below freezing, and the lack of oxygen would make most people struggle for breath. Air-conditioning passes warm air around the cabin. The cabin is kept at high pressure to make it easy to breathe.

Fighting forces

Fighter pilots fly at much higher speeds than passenger jets. They climb and dive very quickly. This puts a great deal of pressure on the pilot's body. If you have been in a car that has stopped very suddenly, you will have felt forces pushing on your body. The same forces act on a pilot's body, but they are much stronger. A pilot climbing out of

F-16 Thunderbird jets put on an impressive display as they fly in formation. As they turn, the pilots feel huge forces.

How high?

Different airplanes fly at different altitudes. This depends on how fast they are and what they are used for.

Space shuttle
More than
115 miles (185 km)

SR-71 Blackbird
More than 80,000
feet (24,500 m)

Concorde
70,000 feet (21,000 m)

Military jet
50,000 feet
(15,000 m)

Jumbo jet
40,000 feet
(12,000 m)

Business jet
24,000 feet (7,500 m)

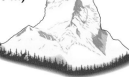
Light aircraft
10,000 feet
(3,000 m)

a dive may feel a force up to nine times the force of gravity (9G) pushing down on his or her body. This force can make the body feel nine times heavier than it normally feels.

Under pressure

When an aircraft dives and climbs, blood rushes to and from the pilot's brain. This would make the pilot feel dizzy if he or she didn't wear a pressure suit. Tubes in the arms, legs, and body of the suit fill with liquid or gas. This squeezes the body to stop the blood rushing to and from the brain and keeps the pilot safe.

THAT'S AMAZING!

The lack of oxygen at high altitude can make fighter pilots feel dizzy and breathless. At very high altitudes, they can fall into a coma or even die. Pilots wear an oxygen mask to help them breathe at high altitudes.

Oxygen mask

Staying Safe

Flying is one of the safest ways to travel, but there are always dangers. Safety gear is on hand to help passengers when accidents happen.

One of the biggest dangers is when ice builds up on the wings. This is because of the freezing temperatures at high altitudes. This increases drag, which slows the plane and makes it difficult to control. Some aircraft have rubber strips on the front of the wings. The strips inflate to break off lumps of ice that have built up. Birds are another danger. They can can get sucked into a jet engine and start a fire.

Crash investigations

Since airplanes fly so high and so quickly, and carry passengers, accidents are usually serious.

Air crash investigators will always investigate the scene to find out the cause of a plane crash.

In an emergency, the pilot will pull on the red handle to trigger the ejector seat.

Air crash investigators always try to figure out what caused the crash to make sure it does not happen again. Air crashes scatter wreckage over a wide area, so the investigators need to collect it. The black box is important. It records details such as speed, altitude, position, and what the pilot was saying when the plane crashed. The black box is tough and can withstand the crash.

Emergency gear

There is a range of equipment in an airplane for when things go wrong. If the pressure inside drops, passengers can breathe using oxygen masks. Inflatable chutes help them to get out if the plane crashes. Inflatable life jackets are available if the plane goes into the sea. Military jets have ejector seats to blast the pilot out of the plane before it crashes. Pilots wear a parachute to float back down to Earth.

TRY FOR YOURSELF

Parachutes

Try this experiment to see how parachutes slow down objects as they fall through the air.

You will need:
- spoon • stopwatch • thread
- piece of paper • sticky tape

1 Drop a spoon. Use a stopwatch to time how long it takes to fall to the floor.
2 Stick the ends of four lengths of thread to the corners of the paper.
3 Wrap the other ends of the thread around a spoon. Tape them in place.
4 Drop the parachute from the same height. How long does the spoon take to fall now?

The parachute increases drag, and the spoon falls more slowly.

Finding the Way

Passenger jets often fly over very long distances to get to their destination. The crew finds the way using a range of navigation equipment.

Most jet planes fly at high altitudes, in all weather, and at night, so pilots cannot always see where they are going. They need tools to help them navigate.

Compasses and altimeters

Compasses point to magnetic north to guide the crew. Compasses on airplanes are mounted on gyroscopes to keep them level when the plane dives or climbs. Altimeters measure altitude.

Satellites and radio

Pilots use GPS (Global Positioning System) satellites to determine a plane's position,

Air traffic controllers direct the flow of airplanes through busy airports.

speed, and direction. Other systems rely on radio waves to help navigate. The Loran (long-range navigation) system picks up radio waves from beacons on the ground, which the plane uses to navigate. Radar (radio

Navigation equipment

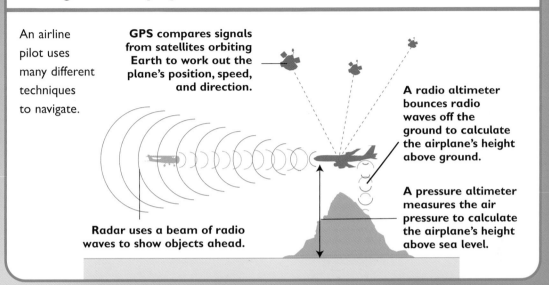

An airline pilot uses many different techniques to navigate.

GPS compares signals from satellites orbiting Earth to work out the plane's position, speed, and direction.

A radio altimeter bounces radio waves off the ground to calculate the airplane's height above ground.

A pressure altimeter measures the air pressure to calculate the airplane's height above sea level.

Radar uses a beam of radio waves to show objects ahead.

detection and ranging) systems send out radio waves to pick up nearby aircraft. The reflections show up on a cockpit screen.

Air traffic control

Airports are busy places. Air traffic controllers guide pilots during takeoff and landing. Every airplane has a transmitter that sends signals to a computer in the control tower. Air traffic controllers use the information to keep the aircraft at a safe distance while they line up in a "stack" to land.

THAT'S AMAZING!

Stealth aircraft are invisible to radar. The surfaces of these planes point in many different directions and scatter radar instead of reflecting it back to enemy planes.

Building a Jet Plane

Jet aircraft take a lot of time and money to build. There are three main stages to aircraft construction: design, construction, and testing.

Jet aircraft fly very high and very quickly. They have to be strong, light, and aerodynamic to cope with the huge forces that build up during flight. Most jet aircraft are designed using computer-aided design (CAD). These computer programs draw detailed pictures of the aircraft. They use complex math to ensure the different parts are up to the job.

The different parts of an aircraft are put together in an assembly hall.

The drawings are then used to produce models that are tested in wind tunnels. Giant fans blow over the model to test the aerodynamics of the aircraft—how well air flows around it.

Building the plane

Airplanes are put together like a giant jigsaw puzzle. Different parts may be manufactured in different places. For example, the wings of the giant Airbus A380 were made in Britain, but the tailplane was made in Spain. All the different parts are then shipped to the assembly hall and put together. The aircraft is then painted and furnished.

Testing stage

Test pilots fly the plane to its limits to see how it copes with the stresses and strains of flight.

Different parts of the Airbus A380 were manufactured in different countries. The aircraft was then assembled in France.

They test a range of emergency situations, such as if the landing gear fails or the engines cut out. They may log thousands of hours of test flights before the plane is approved to fly.

Fast Facts

- A Boeing 747-400 is typically made up of more than six million different parts.
- The fleet of five Airbus A380 aircraft logged more than 4,565 hours during 1,364 test flights before entering service in 2007.

Military Jets

Some military jets have been in service for many years. Others are more recent aircraft that include a range of sophisticated technologies.

The B-2 stealth bomber is one of the most expensive military jet aircraft.

Some military jets have been around for a long time. The B-52 Stratofortress has been used by the United States Air Force (U.S.A.F.) since 1955. The bomber is set to continue in service until at least 2040. The F-4 Phantom is another long-serving aircraft. Launched in 1958, the F-4 Phantom served in the U.S.A.F. until 1996, and it is still used by some countries. For many years, the world's fastest airplane was the SR-71A Blackbird, with a top speed of more than 2,000 miles (3,200 km) per hour. It was retired in the late 1990s after more than 30 years of service.

THAT'S AMAZING!

The jet engines of most military fighters have an afterburner. This is an extra combustion chamber that burns the exhaust gases to produce even more thrust, making the jet even faster.

Record breakers

Military jets continue to set amazing records. The Russian MiG-25 is the world's fastest jet. It can fly at 2,110 miles (3,395 km) per hour. The B-2 Spirit, or "stealth bomber," is one of the world's most expensive military jets. Each one costs a staggering $1.3 billion.

The F-4 Phantom jet is one of the longest-serving jet aircraft.

Pilotless aircraft

Some jet planes fly without pilots because of the huge G forces involved with high-speed flight or the danger of being shot down. Spy planes such as the U.S. RQ-1 Predator are flown deep within enemy territory by remote control. Another advantage of these aircraft is that they can be very small. A U.S.A.F. spy plane called Black Widow is small enough to be carried in a soldier's backpack. It sends back color pictures from a tiny video camera.

The Future of Jet Planes

Jet aircraft of the future will fly faster and more efficiently than modern jets. Passenger jets will carry more passengers much farther, while space-age jets may carry people to Mars.

Developments in passenger jets are aimed at making the planes faster while carrying more passengers and cargo. The huge Airbus A380 "Superjumbos" are the world's largest passenger jets. They can carry between 500 and 800 passengers around 9,500 miles (15,200 km) at a cruising speed of 560 miles (900 km) per hour.

The National Aeronautics and Space Administration (NASA) is developing a supersonic passenger jet that can fly twice as fast as today's jet airliners.

The Joint Strike Fighter will be made of composite materials.

This artist's impression shows what NASA's X-43 hypersonic plane might look like.

Military jets

Most military developments are classified, which means they are top secret. So no one knows what fighter planes of the future will look like. Companies such as Boeing and Lockheed are working on a military jet called the Joint Strike Fighter. This plane will be able to take off and land straight up and down. The Joint Strike Fighter will be made of composites—different materials combined into one strong, lightweight substance. Composites are cheaper than metals. Even so, each plane will still cost $30 million.

Space-age jets

NASA is using space-age technology to develop hypersonic aircraft. Hypersonic

THAT'S AMAZING!

Engineers are developing a new aircraft, with a maple-wing design. They will have no body and look like a giant wing spinning in the air like a leaf. Engineers hope that these maple-wing aircraft might one day take people to Mars.

means flying at more than five times the speed of sound. One project, called Hyper-X, is developing an aircraft with both jet engines and rockets. The airplane will fly at the equivalent of ten times the speed of sound at ground level.

Glossary

aerodynamics: the way air moves over things. The more aerodynamic an object is, the more easily air will pass over it.

afterburner: an extra combustion chamber in a jet engine. The afterburner burns exhaust gases to produce even more thrust.

aileron: a flap on the wing that makes the airplane roll from side to side

airfoil: the name given to the shape of a wing when seen from the side

altitude: an airplane's height above sea level

composites: different materials combined into one strong, lightweight substance

delta wings: triangular-shaped wings that allow airplanes to fly faster than the speed of sound

drag: the rubbing force of the air on the body of the airplane that slows it down

elevator: a flap on the tailplane that makes the airplane pitch up and down

exhaust: the waste gases released from an engine after it has burned the fuel

fuselage: the main body of an airplane

Global Positioning System (GPS): a navigation system that uses satellites to determine the position of an object on Earth

gravity: the force of attraction between different masses

gyroscope: a rotating wheel that can spin freely in all directions

hypersonic: five times the speed of sound

lift: the upward force created by the difference in air pressure above and below the wings of an airplane

navigation: finding your way

pitch: the amount an airplane's nose tips up or down

pressure: the amount of force acting on a surface

pressure suit: a suit worn by pilots of military jets. Tubes in the suit press on the pilot's body to stop blood rushing to and from the brain during steep dives and climbs.

propeller: a metal disk with blades that spin around to push an aircraft through the air

radar: short for radio detection and ranging, radar finds objects by bouncing radio waves off them

roll: the amount an airplane's

wings tip up or down

rudder: movable part on the tailplane that is used to steer an airplane

satellite: an object that orbits Earth. Pilots use satellites to help them find their way.

sonic boom: the shock wave created when an airplane travels faster than the speed of sound

stealth: technology that makes an airplane invisible to radar

subsonic: describes an airplane that flies at speeds below the speed of sound

supersonic: describes an airplane that can travel faster than the speed of sound

throttle: part of an airplane that controls the power of the engine

thrust: the forward force generated by the engine of an airplane

turbine: a set of blades in a drum that spins when driven by the exhaust gases of a jet engine

weight: the force of gravity pulling down on the airplane

yaw: the amount an airplane's nose tips left and right

Further Information

Books to read:

Bledsoe, Karen, and Glen Bledsoe. *Fighter Planes: Fearless Fliers.* Berkeley Heights, NJ: Enslow Publishers, 2007.

Graham, Ian. *Aircraft.* Mankato, MN: Smart Apple Media, 2008.

Web sites to look at:

www.classicjets.org

www.nasa.gov

Museums to visit:

Museum of Flight, Seattle, Washington. www.museumofflight.org

Smithsonian National Air and Space Museum, Washington, D.C. www.nasm.si.edu

Index

accidents 20
aerodynamics 24, 25
ailerons 4, 8, 16
Airbus A380 5, 25, 28
air traffic controllers 23
altimeters 17, 22, 23
altitudes 14, 15, 17, 19, 20, 22
artificial horizon 16, 17

B-52 Stratofortress 26
birds 20
black box 21
Boeing 747 4, 8, 25

cockpit 16, 17
Comet, de Havilland 7
compasses 17, 22
Concorde 14, 15, 19
construction 24
control columns 16, 17

design 24
drag 8, 9, 20, 21

elevators 5, 8, 17
emergency gear 21

F-4 Phantom 26
fly-by-wire 17
Flyer 6

GPS (Global Positioning System) 22, 23
gravity 9, 19
gyroscopes 22

Harrier Jump Jet 13
hypersonic aircraft 29

Joint Strike Fighter 29

landing gear 5, 25
lift force 8, 9
Loran system 22

Messerschmitt Me 262 6, 7
MiG-25 7, 15, 27
military 7, 12, 19, 21, 26, 27, 29

NASA 28, 29
navigation equipment 22, 23

passenger jets 5, 7, 15, 18, 22, 28
pitch 8
pressure suit 19
propellers 6, 12, 13

radar system 4, 22, 23
ramjets 12, 13
rudder 5, 8, 16, 17

sonic booms 15
sound barrier 7, 15
speed of sound 7, 11, 12, 14, 15, 29
spy planes 27
SR-71A Blackbird 26
stealth 23, 27

tailplane 5, 8, 17, 25
thrust 8, 9, 10, 11, 12, 26
turbofans 10, 11, 12, 13
turbojets 12
turboprops 12, 13

weight 8, 9
Whittle, Frank 7
wing shapes 14
Wright, Orville and Wilbur 6

yaw 8